i-SPY

rivers and canals
SPY IT! SCORE IT!

Introduction

Rivers and canals play an important role in the world, not just to humans but to animals and plants as well. In addition to providing water, they have been used for both transport and leisure for hundreds of years. There are many ways to enjoy rivers and canals, and to discover the many different things they have to offer. You might pass over one on a bridge on a car journey, practise riding your bike alongside one, or maybe sail down one when you're on holiday. However you experience these waterways, you'll always find a lot of interesting things to i-SPY as you go.

How to use your i-SPY book

Keep your eyes peeled for the i-SPYs in the book.

If you spy it, score it by ticking the circle or star.

35 POINTS

Items with a star are difficult to spot so you'll have to search high and low to find them.

Once you score 1000 points, send away for your super i-SPY certificate. Follow the instructions on page 64 to find out how.

Boats

Houseboat

This is a boat that is used as a home. Some are permanently moored on rivers and canals, while others are moved from place to place.

20 POINTS

Cabin cruiser

These boats are a popular holiday option as they have sleeping and cooking space inside.

15 POINTS

Ferry

A ferry takes passengers (and sometime vehicles) across or along a river. Sometimes you might have to ring a bell so that the ferryperson knows you're there.

20 POINTS

Boats

Stand-up paddleboard

This water sport, in which you paddle from a standing position on a large floating board, has its origins in the Pacific islands of Hawaii.

 20 POINTS

Kayak

These small, sleek boats are a popular way to explore waterways. They are moved along by double-bladed paddles.

15 POINTS

Canoe

Canoes can carry more people than kayaks so are a good option for families on the water. There is only one blade on the paddle, which means you have to use it on one side and then the other to move along.

 20 POINTS

Punt

These flat-bottomed boats are moved by a punter, who stands at the back and pushes the boat along by using a pole against the river bed. They're most commonly associated with the university cities of Cambridge and Oxford. Sometimes the punter might wear an old-fashioned straw hat, known as a 'boater'.

35 POINTS

TOP SPOT!

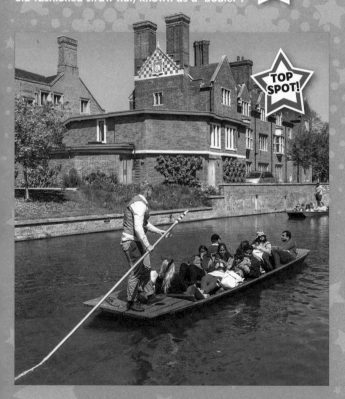

Boats

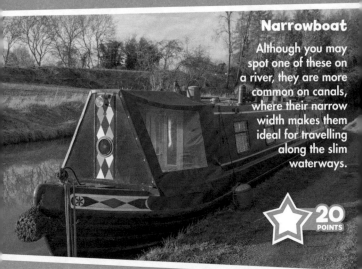

Narrowboat

Although you may spot one of these on a river, they are more common on canals, where their narrow width makes them ideal for travelling along the slim waterways.

20 POINTS

Rowing boat

This type of boat has an oar on either side. You might see a small, wooden boat like the one in this picture, or a longer one that seats rowers in a line and is used for racing.

25 POINTS

RIB

A rigid inflatable boat or RIB can travel very fast. You'll often see them used on wildlife trips or as a safety boat.

30 POINTS

Dutch barge

These look similar to narrowboats but are much wider. As their name suggests, they originally came from the Netherlands.

30 POINTS

Sailing yacht

Yachts are easy to spot by their sails, which enable them to be moved along by the wind.

25 POINTS

Boats

Fishing boat

Lots of different types of boat are used for fishing, but often they'll have an enclosed cabin at the front and be open at the back – ideal for throwing fishing lines over, or for hauling creels (fishing baskets) up.

25 POINTS

Dinghy

These are small, open boats which are often launched from larger boats like yachts and can be used for both rowing and sailing.

30 POINTS

Canada goose

This is the most common type of goose that you'll see by a river in the UK. It has a distinctive black and white face and a very loud honk.

10 POINTS

Greylag goose

The greylag is a large, wild goose with an orange beak, pink legs and grey feathers. It mainly lives in lowland areas.

15 POINTS

Birds and insects

Swan

You might spot these graceful white birds upending themselves, sticking their bottoms up in the air to reach shoots growing on the river bed.

5 POINTS

Mallard duck

The males of our most commonly seen waterbirds have vibrant green heads and yellow beaks, while the females have a brown body and orange beak.

5 POINTS

Mandarin duck

Male mandarin ducks have very colourful plumage (feathers), making the females with their grey feathers seem quite dull in comparison.

25 POINTS

Kingfisher

If you see a flash of turquoise along a riverbank it's most likely to be a kingfisher. They can sometimes be spotted sitting on a branch while they hunt for fish, before swooping into the water to catch them.

35 POINTS

TOP SPOT!

Tufted duck

The males of these black and white ducks are notable for the tuft of feathers at the back of their head, which looks a bit like a little pony tail.

25 POINTS

Grey heron

These tall birds have long necks and sharp, yellow bills – perfect for diving into the water to catch fish.

20 POINTS

Black-headed gull

Despite their name, these gulls actually have a dark brown head – and only in the summer months. The rest of the year, they have a white head.

15 POINTS

Moorhen

Moorhens are black waterbirds. Their red beaks have a yellow tip. You might be surprised by how long their legs are if you see them out of the water!

20 POINTS

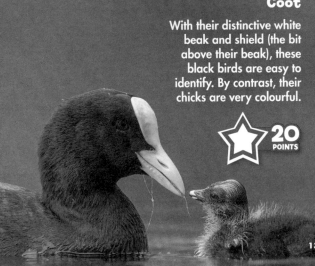

Coot

With their distinctive white beak and shield (the bit above their beak), these black birds are easy to identify. By contrast, their chicks are very colourful.

20 POINTS

13

Birds and insects

Great crested grebe

There are five types of grebe in the UK, but this one is the most distinctive with its long neck and plume of black feathers on its head.

 **25 POINTS**

Cormorant

Look out for this black waterbird on the riverbank, where it will often stand with its wings outstretched to dry them. They are excellent fishers, helped by their webbed feet which allow them to zoom along underwater.

 25 POINTS

Dragonfly

Dragonflies can often be seen zipping around by the water's edge. Their body is made up of ten segments and their big eyes usually meet at the top of their head.

20 POINTS

Damselfly

Smaller and more delicate than dragonflies, damselflies have eyes that sit separately on the top of their head. When resting, they fold their wings in alongside their body.

25 POINTS

Bumblebee

Look for these large, hairy bees from spring till autumn. The best place to spot them is on flowering plants, where they will be collecting pollen.

20 POINTS

15

Birds and insects

Painted lady butterfly

These common butterflies migrate to northern Africa in the colder months, so you're most likely to see them in spring and summer.

20 POINTS

Common blue butterfly

While the upperwings of this small butterfly are a lovely shade of blue, the underside – and often the female's wings – are brown and spotted.

30 POINTS

Red admiral butterfly

This large black butterfly has distinctive red stripes on its wings.

20 POINTS

Scarlet tiger moth

It's easy to mistake this moth for a butterfly, due to its bright colours. While its forewings are usually black with white spots (often with a splash of yellow), its hindwings are a vivid shade of red.

25 POINTS

Grasshopper

These insects are so well camouflaged that it can be hard to spot them. Listen out for the chirping sound they make by rubbing their back legs together, and look for them among long grass.

30 POINTS

Fish and amphibians

Minnow

Look out for shoals of these small fish in freshwater rivers and streams. They often seem to shimmer in the water, making them easy to spot when the light hits them.

15 POINTS

Brown trout

These fish thrive in freshwater rivers that have stony beds. Their young are known as 'fry'.

30 POINTS

Salmon

A number of rivers in Scotland, northern England and Ireland are well known for their salmon. In some places, such as the Falls of Shin in the Highlands, you can see salmon 'leaping' up the waterfalls during the mating season.

30 POINTS

Roach

20 POINTS

This is the most common fish in British rivers and canals and is a popular catch for anglers. Roach often come closer to the surface in warmer weather.

Frog

Frogs like shallow and calm water, so are more likely to be found in streams and canals than rivers.

25 POINTS

Newt

These lizard-like creatures can be hard to spot, partly because they are so well camouflaged with their surroundings, and also because they are small and fast so can dart away quickly.

30 POINTS

Mammals and reptiles

Dormouse

These cute little rodents with big eyes live in hedgerows, where they feed on nuts and fruits. They hibernate for at least six months of the year.

30 POINTS

Otter

These large mammals live all over the UK, but their preference for clean rivers means that Scotland is one of the best places to see them.

30 POINTS

Brown rat

Rats are such adaptable animals that they live pretty much everywhere, so it's not unusual to see them scurrying alongside or even swimming in rivers.

20 POINTS

Mammals and reptiles

Water vole

An endangered animal in the UK, water voles are incredibly hard to spot. They make their burrows (homes) in the riverbanks. Look out for piles of grass and stems that have been nibbled, or for their long, rounded droppings.

35 POINTS

TOP SPOT!

Bat

The best time to spot a bat is just before the sun sets, when they come out to feed. Look out for them swooping through the air, catching insects as they fly.

20 POINTS

Stoat

With their long, thin bodies, these brown and white mammals are excellent swimmers. They're most likely to be spotted by waterways that are close to mountains or woodland.

30 POINTS

Grass snake

There's no need to be scared of these snakes as they are not venomous. Found in England and Wales, you might spot them basking by the water on a sunny day.

25 POINTS

Plants and trees

White willow

You'll often see these beautiful trees leaning over the water from their riverbank position. The name comes from the colour of the underside of their leaves.

20 POINTS

Alder tree

Alders love moist ground so are often found by rivers and streams. Unlike with most trees, their wood doesn't rot when it gets waterlogged.

25 POINTS

Bird cherry tree

This tree is at its most beautiful in late spring when it flowers, and the smell of its blossom is very similar to almonds. The cherries that grow on it are black and bitter – ideal for wildlife but not for humans!

20 POINTS

Common reed

Very common in wetland areas, reeds will cover an area to create golden brown reedbeds. Looking a bit like very tall grass, they are topped by feather-like flowers that start off a dark purple.

15 POINTS

Plants and trees

Meadowsweet

In the summer months you'll see sprays of these white flowers clustered along riverbanks. They're popular with all kinds of insects, from moth caterpillars to ladybirds and bees.

10 POINTS

Bulrush

These tall plants are particularly notable for their brown flowers, which resemble sausages in size and shape. They grow at the water's edge.

10 POINTS

Bladderwort

A carnivorous (meat-eating) water plant with no roots, bladderwort can be easily spotted by its bright yellow flowers. It feeds on creatures such as snails, tadpoles and small fish.

Hemlock water dropwort

Despite being known as the most poisonous plant in the UK, this is very often found along waterways. All parts of the plant are poisonous, so don't eat any of it!

Plants and trees

Apple tree

Look for apple trees growing alongside river paths. In the autumn months, their boughs will become heavy with fruit and you might even be able to pick some.

25 POINTS

Yellow water-lily

This plant is common on still water, so look out for it on canals. The lily pads appear to float on the surface, and the bright yellow flowers appear in the summer months.

20 POINTS

Water mint

Like the herb you can buy in shops, the leaves of water mint can be used in food and drinks. It has pale purple flowers during the summer months.

20 POINTS

Blackberry

Look for blackberry bushes alongside river and canal paths, particularly in late summer when the dark berries can be seen (and picked).
Be warned – they can taste very sour!

15 POINTS

Sloe

The round, purple fruits of the blackthorn bush are at their ripest in autumn. They can be eaten raw but are very sharp – they're better used in things like jellies and syrups.

20 POINTS

Dandelion

The yellow flowers of this common plant turn into fluffy white 'clocks'. It's fun to blow these and watch the seeds scatter.

5 POINTS

River features

Waterfall

A waterfall happens when water in a river or a stream flows over a steep drop. Sometimes this might just be very small, but at other points you might see a dramatic cascade.

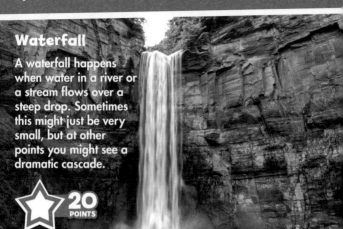

20 POINTS

Rapids

These are areas of fast-flowing, turbulent water – they are great fun for rafting on, but can also be very dangerous.

30 POINTS

Meander

A meander is a large, horse-shoe-like bend in the river. Many rivers have them, due to the way that the land on either side is worn away and then deposited further on.

30 POINTS

River mouth

This point marks the end of a river, where it flows into the sea or a lake. The part of a river that is affected by sea tides is known as an estuary.

30 POINTS

Tributary

A tributary is a watercourse, often a stream or a small river, that flows into a larger river or stream.

15 POINTS

River features

River source

The starting point of a river is its source, which is also known as a headwater. This is often on a hill or a mountain, with the river travelling downhill from there.

35 POINTS

TOP SPOT!

Valley

A valley is formed by the erosion (wearing away) of the land by the river as it runs through it. You can easily identify one – the valley bottom, where the river flows, will be flat, with hills on either side coming down to meet it.

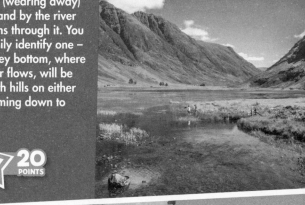

20 POINTS

Gorge

This is a narrow valley with steep, rocky walls rising up on either side. Found in hills and mountains, there are often viewing points where you can stand and appreciate the full size of the gorge.

30 POINTS

River features

Oxbow lake

An oxbow lake is formed when a meander becomes separated from the river flow as the water creates a straighter route to follow.

30 POINTS

Floodplain

The flat land on either side of a river is known as a floodplain. This area floods when the river bursts its banks, usually after very heavy rain.

15 POINTS

Island

Larger rivers may contain islands – some of these may have little more than trees on them, while others are big enough for houses and even for cars to drive onto them.

30 POINTS

Canal features

Lock

In the section of canal between the two sets of lock gates, the water level is raised or lowered by pumps. This enables boats to travel up or downhill.

10 POINTS

Lock-keeper's cottage

You may see a cottage built next to a lock. This would originally have been the home of the lock-keeper, who operated the lock whenever it was needed.

20 POINTS

Towpath

Towpaths were first constructed alongside canals so that horses could pull barges along, but these days they are mainly used by walkers and cyclists.

10 POINTS

Buildings and structures

Watermill

Traditionally used for grinding wheat into flour, watermills were once a common sight on rivers. Many that can be seen today are no longer working, but some have been restored as tourist attractions.

30 POINTS

Harbour or marina

This is a place where boats are docked, usually in a sheltered position that will keep them safe from bad weather.

20 POINTS

Jetty

Often made of wood, a jetty is a landing stage for boats, where they can be tied up or anchored, and from where passengers can walk onto land.

25 POINTS

Boathouse

Boathouses are a bit like large sheds and might have room for just one boat or be large enough to store dozens of rowing boats. You might see a boathouse at the end of a riverside garden.

20 POINTS

Buildings and structures

Castle

Many castles were built overlooking rivers as the water would act like a moat, making it more difficult for enemies to attack. The river would also provide water for the residents of the castle.

20 POINTS

Riverside pub

A riverside pub always makes a scenic place to stop for a refreshment if you are on a walk or a boat trip.

20 POINTS

Docks

These enclosed areas were built to allow ships' cargoes to be loaded and unloaded. Many old docks have now been turned into tourist attractions.

30 POINTS

Dam

A dam acts as a barrier across a river and causes the water to collect behind it in a reservoir. This is then used for water supply or to generate hydroelectricity.

30 POINTS

Barrage

A barrage is a large structure usually made up of a number of gates that can be opened or closed to control the flow of a river.

25 POINTS

Weir

A weir is a small structure built across a river to control the flow or level of the water.

20 POINTS

Bridges

Suspension bridge

A suspension bridge can be identified by the towers that stand at either end, which are joined by curving cables.

Canal bridge

The most common type of bridge that crosses a canal is a humpback bridge – these bridges will often have been built around the time the canal was constructed.

Bascule bridge

Also known as a drawbridge, this type of bridge has one or two parts that lift up, allowing tall boats and ships to pass through.

25 POINTS

Clapper bridge

These are very old bridges, most often found in remote countryside, that are made up of large slabs placed directly on the riverbank or supported by thick piles of other stones and rocks.

30 POINTS

Footbridge

These allow walkers to cross from one side of the water to the other, and are usually made of wood or metal.

10 POINTS

Bridges

Multi-span bridge

A multi-span bridge has one or more supports in between each end. This type of construction means that these bridges can be very long.

15 POINTS

Single-span bridge

A single-span bridge is a simple structure that has support just at the beginning and the end – as a result, they tend to be fairly short in length.

15 POINTS

Swing bridge

A section of this type of bridge can be turned sideways to let water transport through – it makes a kind of swinging motion, hence the name.

30 POINTS

Toll bridge

If you're crossing this type of bridge in a car or other vehicle, you'll need to pay a fee known as a toll. This is often charged to help keep the bridge safe and well maintained.

30 POINTS

Railway bridge

It's not just road traffic and walkers that need to get across rivers and canals, but trains as well. Railway bridges are usually separate to road bridges, and if you're travelling over one on a train you'll often get a great view of the river below.

20 POINTS

Activities

Canoeing

Look out for canoeists on the river, especially during the warmer months. Lots of people find them a fun way to explore.

20 POINTS

Fishing

Anglers use a rod and line with bait on the end to catch fish in rivers and canals.

15 POINTS

Punting

You'll most likely see people punting along the rivers in university cities like Oxford and Cambridge.

30 POINTS

Duck feeding

Lots of people enjoy feeding ducks, but it's an especially fun pastime for young children and toddlers.

 5 POINTS

Cycling

Riverside paths are popular with cyclists because they are often flat and easy for all abilities.

 10 POINTS

Pooh sticks

This is a great game to play on a footbridge over a stream. Everyone throws a stick into the water and the winner is the person whose stick emerges first on the other side.

 20 POINTS

Activities

Dog walking

Riverside paths are lovely places for people to walk dogs. In summer, you might see dogs being let off their leads and jumping into the water to cool off.

5 POINTS

Boat cruise

You'll see lots of different boats sailing down rivers and canals. Some larger boats carry lots of passengers on a cruise to take in the sights along the way.

25 POINTS

Paddling

On a hot day, you might spot people paddling in the shallow waters at the river's edge.

20 POINTS

Swimming

River swimming is often also called 'wild swimming'. You'll most likely see people doing it on quieter stretches of water, away from towns and cities.

20 POINTS

Ice-cream van

Sometimes an ice-cream van will park up by a river or canal during the summer months so that people can enjoy a tasty treat while they enjoy the view.

15 POINTS

ICE CREAM

Activities

Whitewater rafting

This adventure sport involves four to eight people in an inflatable raft that is paddled down rapids (fast-flowing water) in a river. It's exciting but beginners should start with Class I rapids, which are the easiest.

35 POINTS

TOP SPOT!

Picnic

Rivers and canals often provide lots of pleasant places to relax, so you may see people sitting on blankets or folding chairs enjoying a picnic.

15 POINTS

River tubing

This adventure sport involves floating down a river on a tube (a kind of big ring that you sit in). Tubers wear a helmet, life jacket and wetsuit to help keep them safe and warm.

30 POINTS

Famous river landmarks

Ironbridge Gorge

This deep gorge in Shropshire is famous for its red bridge, which was the world's first iron bridge. The gorge and the nearby town both take their names from the bridge, which crosses the River Severn.

25 POINTS

Humber Bridge

When it was built in 1981, this was the longest single-span suspension bridge in the world. Today it is only the eighth longest, but more than ten million vehicles use it every year!

20 POINTS

Glenfinnan Railway Viaduct

This beautiful railway viaduct over the River Finnan in northwest Scotland is most famous these days for its appearance in many of the Harry Potter films.

25 POINTS

Forth Bridge

This striking red steel structure is one of three bridges that cross the Forth Estuary to the northwest of Edinburgh.

20 POINTS

Famous river landmarks

Gateshead Millennium Bridge

The world's only tilt bridge, this semi-circular structure leans to one side to allow ships on the River Tyne to pass underneath.

20 POINTS

Millennium Bridge

Tees Transporter Bridge

This unusual bridge in northeast England transports people and vehicles across the River Tees in a gondola that is suspended above the water. Up to nine cars can be carried at one time.

25 POINTS

Tower Bridge

One of London's most famous sights, the middle of this bascule bridge opens up to allow river traffic to pass underneath. The walkways at the top of the bridge provide fantastic views of the city and the River Thames – though you'll need a good head for heights!

10 POINTS

Thames Barrier

The barriers of this impressive system help to prevent flooding in London. The barriers are closed at high tide and then opened at low tide. You can see it in the River Thames near Woolwich, in southeast London.

15 POINTS

Famous river landmarks

Bridge of Sighs

This ornate covered bridge is part of St John's College in Cambridge. Crossing the River Cam, it was built in 1831 to connect the college's older buildings with its new development on the west side and was originally known as 'New Bridge'.

30 POINTS

Clifton Suspension Bridge

This imposing bridge above the Avon Gorge in Bristol took 33 years to complete. It was designed by Isambard Kingdom Brunel, a civil engineer who built many well-known structures in the nineteenth century.

25 POINTS

Famous canal landmarks

Anderton Boat Lift

Built in 1875, this impressive structure is one of only two boat lifts in the UK. It lifts boats up by 15 metres so they can transfer from the River Weaver to the Trent and Mersey Canal in Cheshire.

25 POINTS

Standedge Tunnel

This tunnel on the Huddersfield Narrow Canal is not only the longest in the country, it's also the deepest and the highest. At three and a half miles long, it goes right underneath the Pennine mountains.

25 POINTS

Famous canal landmarks

Pontcysyllte Aqueduct

The highest canal aqueduct in the world, this structure enables boats on the Llangollen Canal to travel over the River Dee in northeast Wales.

25 POINTS

Neptune's Staircase

Part of the Caledonian Canal in the Scottish Highlands, this succession of eight locks is the longest staircase lock in Britain.

30 POINTS

Falkirk Wheel

This amazing piece of engineering is the world's only rotating boat lift. It enables boats to travel from the Firth and Clyde Canal to the Union Canal, effectively lifting them up into the sky in the process.

20 POINTS

Famous rivers

River Severn

The UK's longest river begins in mid-Wales (where it is called *Afon Hafren*) and ends at the Severn Estuary, which opens into the Bristol Channel.

 15 POINTS

River Thames

Perhaps most famous for flowing through London, the Thames is also known as the Isis along the stretch from its source (in the Cotswolds) to the point in Oxfordshire where it meets the River Thame.

 10 POINTS

River Trent

This river is particularly notable for flowing north (it's more common for rivers to flow south). It ends at the Humber Estuary near the city of Kingston upon Hull. **15 POINTS**

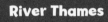

Famous rivers

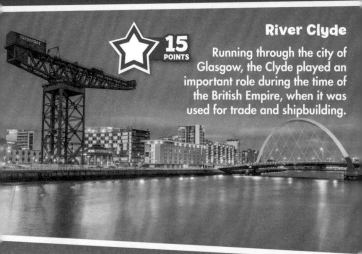

River Clyde

15 POINTS

Running through the city of Glasgow, the Clyde played an important role during the time of the British Empire, when it was used for trade and shipbuilding.

River Great Ouse

25 POINTS

There are a number of rivers with 'Ouse' in their name – the word is thought to come from the Celtic word for water – but this is the longest of them. It flows from Northamptonshire to Norfolk, where it meets the North Sea.

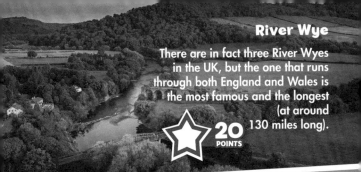

River Wye

There are in fact three River Wyes in the UK, but the one that runs through both England and Wales is the most famous and the longest (at around 130 miles long).

20 POINTS

River Avon

This river is also known as the Bristol Avon or the Lower Avon to distinguish it from the eight other rivers with the same name. It starts in Gloucestershire.

15 POINTS

River Mersey

This river is famous for the ferries that sail across it between the city of Liverpool and the Wirral peninsula. A famous song – 'Ferry Cross the Mersey' – was even written about it.

15 POINTS

Famous rivers

River Tyne

A major river in the northeast of England, the Tyne is especially famous for separating the cities of Newcastle and Gateshead.

15 POINTS

River Lagan

This Northern Irish river flows for 53 miles from Slieve Croob mountain to Belfast Lough. Seals are sometimes seen swimming in the water.

30 POINTS

Famous canals

Llangollen Canal

This canal crosses the England–Wales border. The Llangollen end of it can only be done by horse-drawn boat as it is too narrow for normal canal boats.

30 POINTS

Caledonian Canal

This canal in the Scottish Highlands connects the east and west coasts. Along its length there are four lochs and 29 locks.

30 POINTS

Grand Union Canal

The UK's longest canal links Birmingham and London, travelling through the countryside between the two cities for 137 miles.

20 POINTS

Famous canals

Monmouthshire & Brecon Canal

This 35-mile canal is often considered the prettiest in the UK, partly because it runs through the Brecon Beacons National Park in Wales for much of its length.

30 POINTS

Grand Canal

Connecting the Irish capital of Dublin with the River Shannon, this canal was used for transporting goods across the country until 1960. Now, like many canals, it is mainly used for recreation.

25 POINTS

Index

activities 44–49
alder tree 24
Anderton boat lift 55
apple tree 28
barrage 39
bascule bridge 40
bat 23
bird cherry tree 25
birds and insects 9–17
blackberry 29
black-headed gull 12
bladderwort 27
boat cruise 46
boathouse 37
boats 3–8
Bridge of Sighs 54
bridges 40–43
brown rat 21
brown trout 18
buildings and structures 36–39
bulrush 26
bumblebee 15
cabin cruiser 3
Caledonian Canal 61
Canada goose 9
canal bridge 40
canal features 35
canoe 4
canoeing 44
castle 38
clapper bridge 41
Clifton suspension Bridge 54
common blue butterfly 16
common reed 26
coot 13
cormorant 14
cycling 45
dam 39
damselfly 15
dandelion 29
dinghy 8

docks 38
dog walking 46
dormouse 20
dragonfly 15
duck feeding 45
Dutch barge 7
Falkirk Wheel 56
famous canal landmarks 55–56
famous canals 61–62
famous river landmarks 50–54
famous rivers 57–60
ferry 3
fish and amphibians 18–19
fishing 44
fishing boat 8
floodplain 34
footbridge 41
Forth Bridge 51
frog 19
Gateshead Millennium Bridge 52
Glenfinnan Railway Viaduct 51
gorge 33
Grand Canal 62
Grand Union Canal 61
grass snake 23
grasshopper 17
great crested grebe 14
grey heron 12
greylag goose 9
harbour 36
hemlock water dropwort 27
houseboat 3
Humber Bridge 50
ice-cream van 47
Ironbridge Gorge 50
island 34

jetty 37
kayak 4
kingfisher 11
Llangollen Canal 61
lock 35
lock-keeper's cottage 35
mallard duck 10
mammals and reptiles 20–23
mandarin duck 10
marina 36
meadowsweet 26
meander 31
minnow 18
Monmouthshire & Brecon Canal 62
moorhen 13
multi-span bridge 42
narrowboat 6
Neptune's Staircase 56
newt 19
otter 21
oxbow lake 34
paddling 47
painted lady butterfly 16
picnic 49
plants and trees 24–29
Pontcysyllte Aqueduct 56
pooh sticks 45
punt 5
punting 44
railway bridge 43
rapids 30
red admiral butterfly 17
RIB 7
River Avon 59
River Clyde 58
river features 30–35
River Great Ouse 58
River Lagan 60

River Mersey 59
river mouth 31
River Severn 57
river source 32
River Thames 57
River Trent 57
river tubing 49
River Tyne 60
River Wye 59
riverside pub 38
roach 19
rowing boat 6
sailing yacht 7
salmon 18
scarlet tiger moth 17
single-span bridge 42
sloe 29
Standedge tunnel 55
stand-up paddleboard 4
stoat 23
suspension bridge 40
swan 10
swimming 47
swing bridge 42
Tees Transporter Bridge 52
Thames Barrier 53
toll bridge 43
Tower Bridge 53
towpath 35
tributary 31
tufted duck 12
valley 33
water mint 28
water vole 22
waterfall 30
watermill 36
weir 39
white willow 24
whitewater rafting 48
yellow water-lily 28

i-SPY

How to get your i-SPY certificate and badge

Let us know when you've become a super-spotter with 1000 points and we'll send you a special certificate and badge!

Here's what to do:

- Ask an adult to check your score.

- Apply for your certificate at www.collins.co.uk/i-SPY (if you are under the age of 13 we'll need a parent or guardian to do this).

- We'll email your certificate and post you a brilliant badge!